yukismart.com/b/650086

1

one

один
odyn

pineapple

ананас
ananas

guitar

гітара
hitara

2

two

два
dva

dinosaurs

динозаври
dynozavry

twins

близнюки
blyzniuky

3

three

три
try

starfishes

морські зірки
morski zirky

peaches

персики
persyky

4

four

чотири
chotyry

cherries

черешні
chereshni

robots

роботи
roboty

five

п'ять
p'iat

fingers

пальці
paltsi

pencils

олівці
olivtsi

6

six

шість
shist

candies

цукерки
tsukerky

hearts

серця
sertsia

7

seashells

морські раковини

morski rakovyny

blocks

кубики

kubyky

8

eight

вісім
visim

ants

мурахи
murakhy

flowers

квіти
kvity

9

nine

дев'ять
dev'iat

fishes

риби
ryby

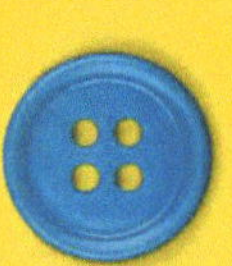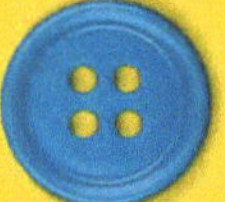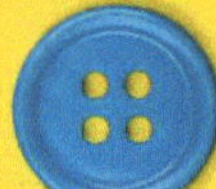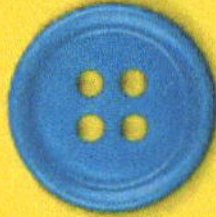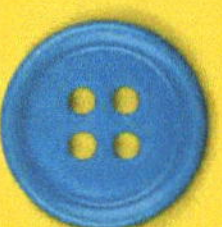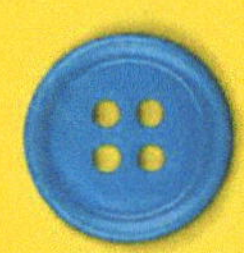

buttons

ґудзики
gudzyky

10

ten

десять
desiat

candles

свічки
svichky

eggs

яйця
iaitsia

even

парне
parne

odd

непарне
neparne

whole

ціле
tsile

half

половина
polovyna

red

червоний
chervonyi

umbrella

парасолька
parasolka

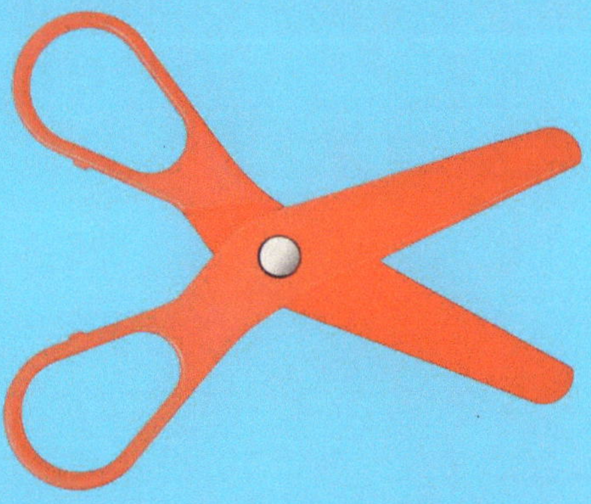

scissors

ножиці
nozhytsi

yellow

жовтий
zhovtyi

banana

банан
banan

cheese

сир
syr

green
зелений
zelenyi

vegetables
овочі
ovochi

bottle
бутилка
butylka

gray

сірий
siryi

carpet

килим
kylym

feather

перо
pero

orange

помаранчевий
pomaranchevyi

pumpkin

гарбуз
harbuz

orange juice

апельсиновий сік
apelsynovyi sik

white
білий
bilyi

cup
чашка
chashka

envelope
конверт
konvert

black

чорний
chornyi

glasses

окуляри
okuliary

shirt

сорочка
sorochka

brown

коричневий
korychnevyi

violin

скрипка
skrypka

cake

тістечко
tistechko

blue

синій

synii

swim shorts

купальні шорти

kupalni shorty

swimming goggles

окуляри для плавання

okuliary dlia plavannia

pink

рожевий
rozhevyi

ice cream

морозиво
morozyvo

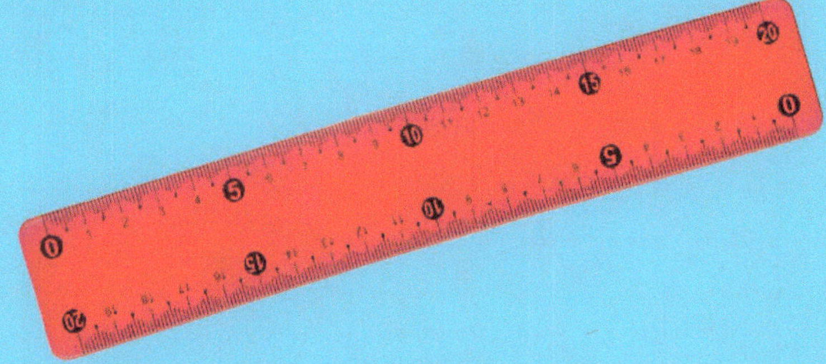

ruler

лінійка
liniika

purple

фіолетовий
fioletovyi

dice

гральні кості
hralni kosti

fan

віяло
viialo

light colors

світлі кольори

svitli kolory

dark colors

темні кольори

temni kolory

circle

коло
kolo

square

квадрат
kvadrat

star

зірка
zirka

heart

серце
sertse

crescent

півмісяць

pivmisiats

triangle

трикутник

trykutnyk

rectangle

прямокутник

priamokutnyk

oval

овал

oval

drop

крапля
kraplia

cross

хрест
khrest

cube

куб
kub

sphere

сфера
sfera

ring

кільце
kiltse

trefoil

трилисник
trylysnyk

cylinder

циліндр
tsylindr

cone

конус
konus

line

лінія
liniia

arrow

стрілка
strilka

dots

крапки
krapky

zigzag

зигзаг
zyhzah

curve

крива
kryva

spiral

спіраль
spiral

draw

малювати
maliuvaty

paint

фарбувати
farbuvaty

count

рахувати
rakhuvaty

write

писати
pysaty

small

маленький
malenkyi

big

великий
velykyi

mouse

миша
mysha

elephant

слон
slon

short

коро́ткий
korotkyi

long

до́вгий
dovhyi

worm

черв'я́к
cherv'iak

snake

змія́
zmiia

thin

тонкий
tonkyi

thick

товстий
tovstyi

empty

пустий
pustyi

full

повний
povnyi

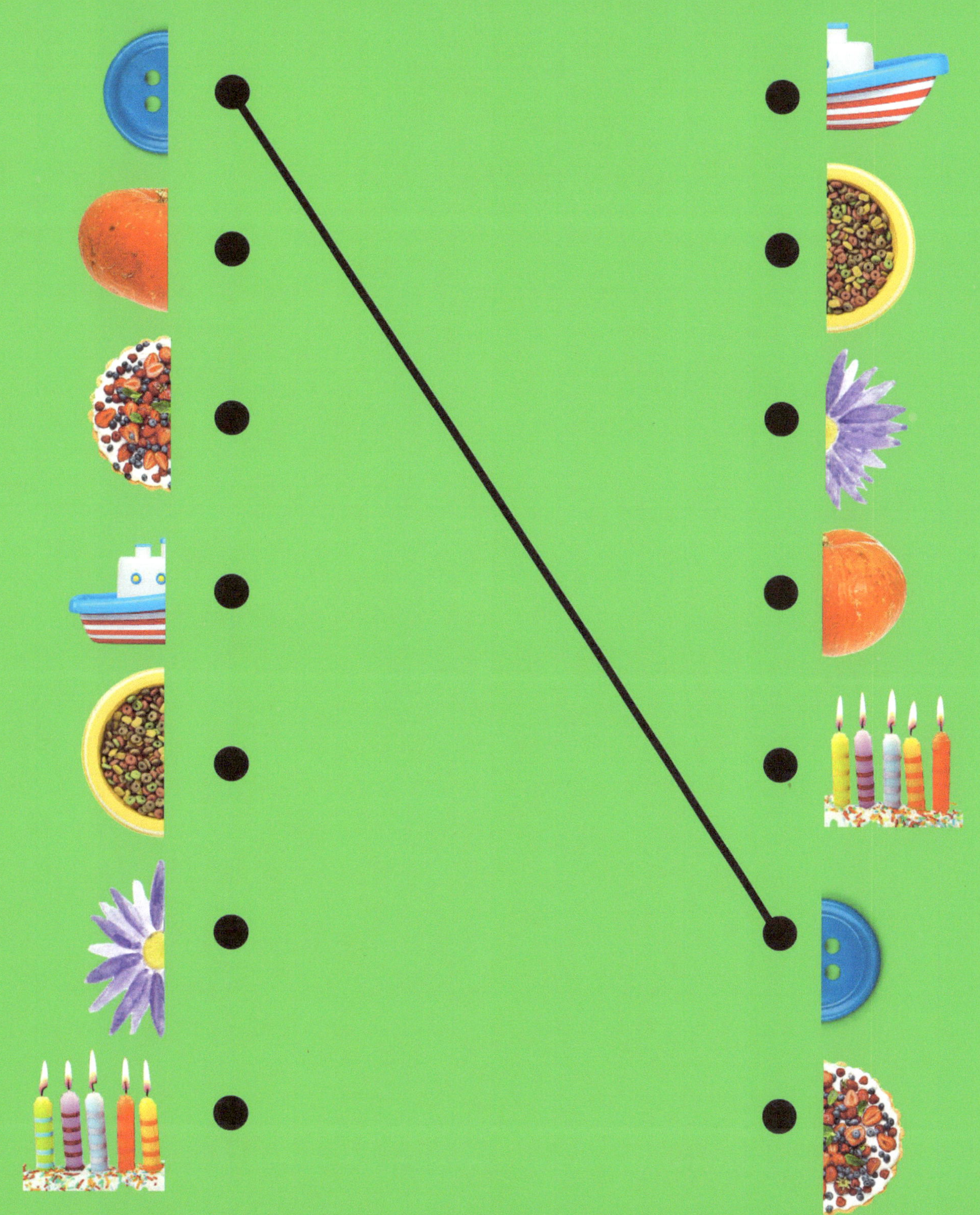